SECRETS OF SPACE

THE SUN AND THE SOLAR SYSTEM

Franklyn M. Branley

Series Editor:
Arthur Upgren, Professor of Astronomy
Wesleyan University

NEW HANOVER COUNTY
PUBLIC LIBRARY
201 CHESTNUT STREET
WILMINGTON, NC 28401

Twenty-First Century Books

Brookfield, Connecticut

Twenty-First Century Books
A division of The Millbrook Press, Inc.
2 Old New Milford Road
Brookfield, Connecticut 06804

Printed in the United States of America

Created and produced in association with Blackbirch Graphics, Inc.

Photo Credits
Cover and p. 4: ©NASA; pp. 6, 32, 46, 48: ©NASA/Peter Arnold, Inc.; p. 12: ©Julian Baum/Science Photo Library/Photo Researchers, Inc.; p. 14: ©J. Baum and N. Henbest/Science Photo Library /Photo Researchers, Inc.; p. 16: ©David Hardy/Science Photo Library/Photo Researchers, Inc.; p. 18: North Wind Picture Archives; p. 22: ©European Space Agency/Science Photo Library/Photo Researchers, Inc.; pp. 26, 53: ©NASA/Science Source/Photo Researchers, Inc.; p. 37: ©Dennis di Cicco/Peter Arnold, Inc.; p. 38: ©NASA/Mark Marten/Photo Researchers, Inc.; p. 40: ©Dr. F. Espenak/Science Photo Library/Photo Researchers, Inc.; p. 44: ©John Foster/Science Source/Photo Researchers, Inc.; p. 51: ©Chris Bjornberg/Photo Researchers, Inc.; p. 52: ©MSSSO, ANU/Science Photo Library/Photo Researchers, Inc.; p. 54: ©Photo Researchers, Inc.; p. 56: ©W. F. Kaufmann/JPL/Science Source/Photo Researchers, Inc.

Artwork by Blackbirch Graphics, Inc.

Library of Congress Cataloging-in-Publication Data

Branley, Franklyn Mansfield
    The sun and the solar system / Franklyn M. Branley.
        p.   cm. — (Secrets of space)
    Includes bibliographical references and index.
    Summary: Discusses the sun and the solar system, comparing how they were perceived in earlier times with what is known about them now.
    ISBN 0-8050-4475-2
    1. Solar system—Juvenile literature. 2. Sun—Juvenile literature. 3. Planets—Juvenile literature. [1. Solar system. 2. Sun.] I. Title. II. Series.
QB501.3.B73   1996
523.2—dc20   96-2836
                                                                                                      CIP
                                                                                                      AC

TABLE OF CONTENTS

INTRODUCTION

Humans have always been fascinated by space, but it has been only since the 1950s that technology has allowed us to actually travel beyond our Earth's atmosphere to explore the universe. What riches of knowledge this space exploration has brought us! All of the planets except Pluto have been mapped extensively, if not completely. Among the planets, only Pluto has not been visited by a space probe, and that will likely change soon. Men have walked on the Moon, and many of the satellites of Jupiter, Saturn, Uranus, and even Neptune have been investigated in detail.

We have learned the precise composition of the Sun and the atmospheres of the planets. We know more about comets, meteors, and asteroids than ever before. And many scientists now think there may be other forms of life in our galaxy and beyond.

In the *Secrets of Space* series, we journey through the wondrous world of space: our solar system, our galaxy, and our universe. It is a world seemingly without end, a world of endless fascination.

—Arthur Upgren
Professor of Astronomy
Wesleyan University

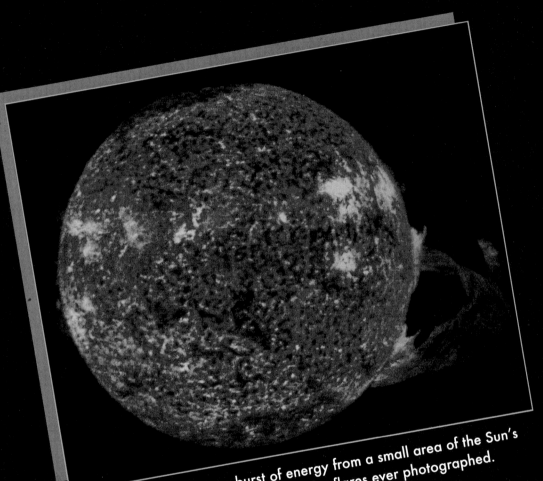

A solar flare is a temporary burst of energy from a small area of the Sun's surface. This is one of the most spectacular flares ever photographed.

CHAPTER 1

THE SUN AND THE PLANETS

The Sun is the source of all the light, heat, and other forms of energy (except nuclear energy) that we have on planet Earth. If the Sun stopped shining, all life on Earth would disappear—every single animal, plant, insect, bird, and fish. Earth would become a dead planet.

The Sun is a star, but there are stars that are thousands of times larger and thousands of times brighter. Our Sun is a dwarf—one of the smaller stars in the universe. Yet, while the Sun is not a giant among stars, it is huge in comparison to Earth. Earth's diameter is 7,926 miles (12,756 kilometers); in contrast, the Sun's diameter is 865,400 miles (1,392,429 kilometers). If Earth were the size of a dime—about 0.5 inch (1.27 centimeters) across—the Sun, in relative terms, would measure about

50 inches (127 centimeters) across. Put another way, more than 1 million Earths could fit inside the Sun.

The Sun is the closest star to Earth. The distance between them, however, is still huge—approximately 93 million miles (150 million kilometers). Ninety-three million miles is almost unimaginable to us, but it is actually a short distance in the scheme of the universe. Beyond the Sun, the star that is next nearest to Earth is so far away—about 26 trillion miles (42 trillion kilometers)—that it takes its light more than 4 years to reach us.

From the Earth, the Sun appears to have a solid surface. But this is an illusion created by the vast distance between the two bodies. The Sun is made completely of gases. About 99 percent of it is composed of hydrogen and helium.

You would think that because the Sun is entirely gaseous, it would have little mass, or matter. But that is not the case. Let us say that the mass of the entire Earth equals 1—that is, all the water, rocks, soil, steel, iron, and everything else combined. Using that point of reference, the mass of the Sun is 330,000— thousands of times greater than the mass of Earth!

How Stars Are Born

Scattered among the stars are huge clouds of gas. Some of these gas clouds are millions, and some are even billions, of miles across. Many are composed completely of hydrogen. Others have helium and traces of other elements, such as iron, silicon, boron, and barium. All of these elements are in gaseous form.

The gases are drawn together whenever a cloud is agitated— perhaps by another cloud of gases that has been ejected from an

Measuring Distances in Space

The Sun and the Earth are approximately 93 million miles apart. Another way of describing this distance is to say that the Sun is slightly more than 8 light-minutes from us. One light-minute is the distance that light travels in one minute in a vacuum. So, the light from the Sun takes about 8 minutes to travel to Earth. Put another way, the light striking Earth right now left the Sun 8 minutes ago. Light travels at 186,282 miles per second. So, if you figure out the number of seconds there are in 8 minutes (8 minutes x 60 seconds = 480 seconds) and multiply that number by 186,282, you will find that in 8 minutes, light will travel close to 89 million miles (480 seconds x 186,282 miles per second = 89,415,360 miles). Since the distance from Earth to the Sun is slightly more than 8 light-minutes, the answer is approximated as 93 million miles. (If you used 8.3 light-minutes to calculate, you would get 92.8 million miles.)

exploding star. Such a cloud may be moving thousands of miles per second. Over a period of hundreds of thousands of years, the gases become more dense, packing closer and closer together. This phenomenon—called accretion—is caused by the pull of gravity. The packing of the molecules raises the temperature of the gases. The temperature rises higher and higher, reaching 1 million degrees Fahrenheit (°F) (555,000°C) and more.

When temperatures reach 76 million °F (42 million °C), hydrogen begins to fuse. In this process, hydrogen atomic nuclei (one nucleus is the core of an atom) join together. When this occurs, a tremendous amount of energy is given off, and a nuclear fusion reaction results. Now the cloud of gas becomes a new star—a mass of gases that produces energy in the form of

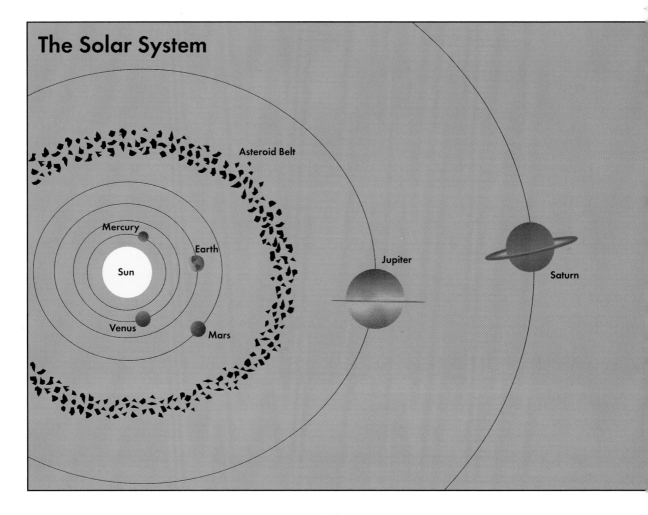

The Solar System

heat and light. The reaction becomes self-sustaining; the fusion in the star may continue for billions of years.

The Sun, for example, has been shining for an estimated 4.5 billion years, and it will probably continue to shine for another 5 billion years. When the Sun stops shining, or emitting energy, all life on Earth will cease to exist.

Today, most of the gas in the Sun is hydrogen, but a large part of it—perhaps 10 to 20 percent—is helium. For every 1 million hydrogen atoms in the Sun, there are approximately

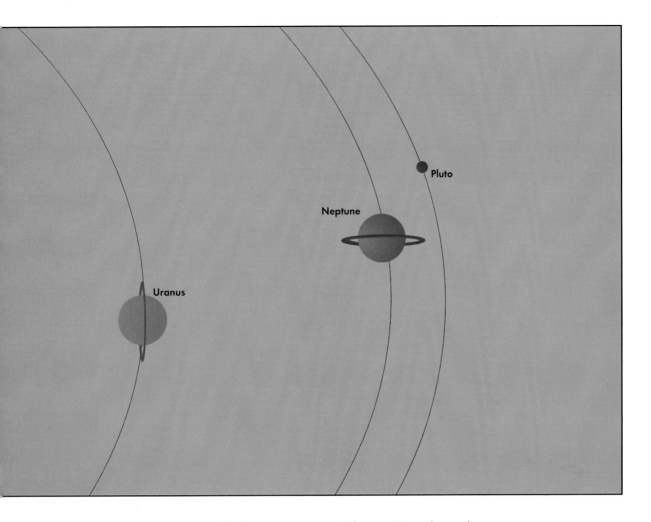

100,000 to 200,000 helium atoms. About 70 other elements found on Earth, including aluminum, calcium, carbon, nickel, and nitrogen, have also been detected in the Sun.

The Origin of the Planets

When a tremendous gas cloud packed together to become the Sun, some of its mass—less than 1 percent—was left over. Many of these leftover gases then condensed. As they mixed

The Origin of the Universe: The Big Bang

We believe that ours is an explosive universe. Somewhere between 13 billion and 20 billion years ago (scientists are sharply divided over just how *many* billions of years ago) a central core that contained all the energy of the universe exploded. This is called the Big Bang—the greatest cataclysm of all time. How the central core got there and what came before it are unknown and may never be known.

In this picture, an artist portrays the Big Bang at a time when giant clouds of gas (the white spots) had already started condensing into what would become galaxies.

The energy in this core, or cosmic fireball, was released during the Big Bang. It then expanded rapidly and cooled. In the process, matter was formed into subatomic particles and then into the simplest of atoms in gaseous states: hydrogen, deuterium (heavy hydrogen), and helium.

Great masses of these gases formed, measuring hundreds of light-years across, consisting mostly of hydrogen. After multiple collisions, the gases packed together and became dense enough to create stars, galaxies, and ultimately the planets, their satellites, and all the other celestial objects that we know about today.

What lies beyond the universe as we know it is still a mystery that is of intense interest to astronomers. There may be another universe. And our universe may even be just one of untold numbers of universes.

together, they reacted chemically with one another, which changed their composition. Eventually, the mixture became solid debris. These solid materials collided and then separated from one another, only to join together again.

Through this action, miniscule particles became slightly larger—they gained in mass. They also gained in gravity (the more massive a body is, the greater its gravity). In turn, this increased gravity attracted yet other tiny particles, again increasing the mass of its body, and, thus, its gravity. And so even more particles were attracted, or collected, together. Eventually some bodies became massive enough to be called planets. In the system of our Sun, which is called the solar system, nine planets formed through this process, including Earth, our home planet.

Not all the leftover debris formed into planets. Some of the debris remained in the form of small bodies called asteroids. Some other material remained in yet smaller bodies known as comets or meteoroids. Much of the debris remained microscopic in size and formed into a vast cloud surrounding the solar system. Even now, particles in that cloud join together to produce comets. As they travel, comets can occasionally be seen from Earth.

Together, the Sun, the nine planets, asteroids, meteoroids, comets, and the cloud make up the solar system. More than 99 percent of the mass of the solar system is contained in the Sun. That mass gives the Sun tremendous gravity, enough to hold the entire system together. The rest of the mass of the system, including the planets, moves around the Sun, held in orbit by its gravity.

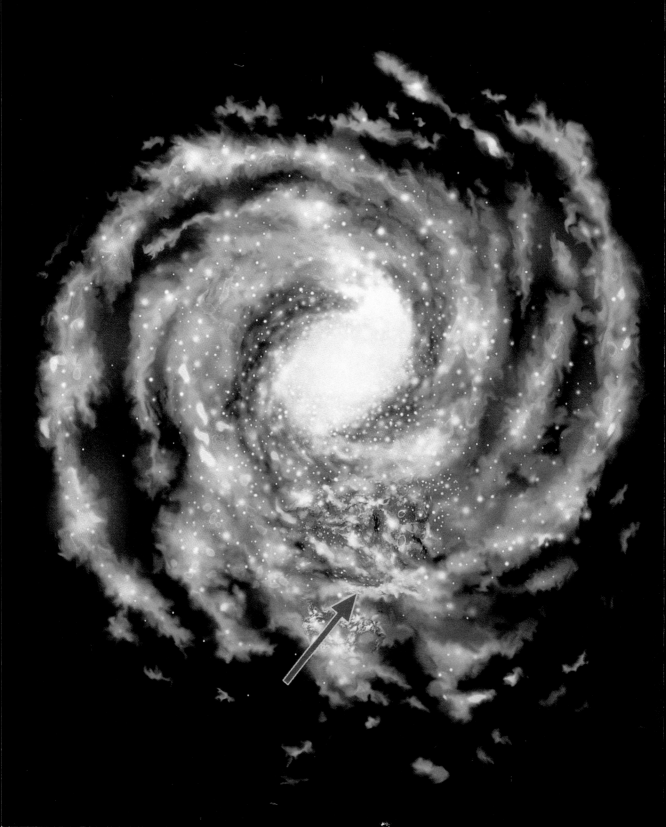

To us, of course, Earth is the most important planet. But in terms of the solar system, Earth is not particularly significant, since several other bodies are much larger. And like the other eight planets, Earth is ultimately made up of space debris.

Location of the Solar System

When you look into the sky on a clear night, away from city lights and haze, you can see 2,000 or 3,000 stars. They are but a small part of the vast collection of stars in our galaxy, called the Milky Way, the celestial formation in which our solar system is located.

Ours is a galaxy of more than 100 billion stars. Most astronomers believe that these multitudes of stars are arranged in a rather flat disk with a central bulge, appearing like two fried eggs back to back.

Earth—in fact, the entire solar system—appears as just a tiny dot in this galactic formation, located nearer to the edge than the center. The Milky Way galaxy is so named because of the milklike band that we can observe as we look out from Earth on a very clear night. The Milky Way is only a medium-size galaxy. Some galaxies are much larger, with thousands of billions of stars. Scientists estimate that there may be close to 100 billion galaxies! All of these galaxies together, and everything in them, make up our universe.

The Milky Way is a spiral galaxy, its arms filled with clouds of molecules and dust. The arrow in this image points to our Sun.

For centuries, people believed that everything revolved around the Earth.
In fact, Earth and the other planets in the solar system circle the Sun.

CHAPTER 2

OUR KNOWLEDGE OF THE SOLAR SYSTEM GROWS

Two thousand years ago, and no doubt even thousands of years before that, people were convinced that Earth was the most important part of the universe. Claudius Ptolemy, a second-century A.D. Greek astronomer, held a geocentric view—that Earth was the very center of the universe. Ptolemy said that everything that could be observed in the sky—the Sun, the Moon, the stars, and the other planets that were then known— moved around Earth. People believed that Earth stood still, that it did not move through space, and that it did not rotate. Since Earth was the center of the universe, it was stationary.

Copernican Theory

Copernicus caused a huge controversy by claiming that the Earth moved around the Sun.

Ptolemy wrote books about his ideas that were studied and believed for more than a thousand years. Then, in 1543, a Polish astronomer and Roman Catholic Church official named Nicolaus Copernicus said that Ptolemy was wrong, that the Earth was not the center of the universe. This was considered a terrible, even unholy, thing to say, because the Church taught Ptolemy's theory. Since Copernicus himself was a leader of the Church, his influence on people's beliefs was thought to be especially dangerous.

Despite opposition from powerful religious and political leaders of the time, Copernicus insisted that the Earth moved—indeed, that it went around the Sun. He argued that Earth was not the center of the universe—not even the center of the solar system. The Sun, he said, was at the center.

This is called the heliocentric theory. Copernicus could not scientifically prove his ideas, though, so they were not widely accepted in his time.

In science, there are often many different theories to explain a single thing. But unless these theories can be proved by formal experiments or by other kinds of repeated observations, they will remain theories rather than facts. This does not mean, however, that theories are not of value: Whether proven or not, they get people thinking. By sparking thought, experimentation, and observation, a theory is often eventually added as fact to our store of knowledge.

That is what happened with the Copernican theory. For more than 100 years, people argued about the solar system. This debate was considered in such opposition to religious authority that some churches actually forbade discussion of Copernicus's ideas, sometimes even by threat of death.

Giordano Bruno, a cleric of the Roman Catholic Church who lived from about 1548 to 1600, taught Copernican theory. For doing so, he was tried by a Church court and convicted of heresy—spreading teachings that did not follow those of the Church. His sentence was to be burned at the stake.

Somewhat later, in the early 1600s, Galileo Galilei, an Italian astronomer and physicist who lived from 1564 to 1642, also taught Copernican theory. As it had done with Bruno, the Church brought Galileo to trial and found him guilty of heresy. Galileo's sentence was not as severe as Bruno's had been—he was imprisoned in his own home. The punishment was effective, however. Galileo was no longer allowed to teach. Thus, he could not spread his "dangerous" ideas.

Galileo, Bruno, and many others were persuaded so strongly by Copernicus's radical theories about the nature of our universe that they were willing to suffer, even to die, to defend what they believed to be the truth.

Gradually, the ideas of these great scientists came to be accepted as more and more people started to believe in them. Today, the ideas are generally viewed as fact in the world of science. We can now prove scientifically that the Sun is the center of our solar system and that the Sun's gravity holds this system together.

In the years after Copernicus, new questions surfaced: What makes the planets go around the Sun, and why don't they fly off into space? Many astronomers and other scientists contributed to answering these questions.

Planetary Motion

One of these contributors was a Danish astronomer named Tycho Brahe. Brahe, who lived from 1546 to 1601, was a very careful observer. By watching the night sky, he recorded the motions of the planets, especially Venus, Mars, and Jupiter. He also showed that comets are space bodies and not weather phenomena, as had been widely believed.

One of Brahe's pupils was Johannes Kepler, a German astronomer (1571–1630). Kepler was greatly intrigued by Brahe's charts of planetary motion. After studying them carefully, Kepler concluded that the planets did not travel in circles, as Copernicus had said, but in more oval patterns called ellipses. Kepler also discovered that the Sun exerted a major gravitational pull on the planets.

Kepler's theory implied that the distance between each planet and the Sun kept continually changing. His theory also meant that when a planet was closest to the Sun in its orbit, the strength of the pull increased and the planet moved most rapidly. When it was at its farthest distance from the Sun, the planet moved most slowly.

Kepler's theory is supported by what we have learned about the varying speeds of Earth. Today, we know that the mean, or average, speed at which the Earth travels around the Sun is 66,600 miles (107,200 kilometers) per hour. When it is closest to the Sun, the Earth moves a bit faster, and when it is farthest away from the Sun, the Earth travels at a somewhat slower speed.

Newton and the Role of Gravity in Space

About 50 years after Kepler set forth his ideas, Isaac Newton, an English astronomer, made one of the most significant and far-reaching scientific discoveries of all time. Newton, who lived from 1642 to 1727, found that everything in the universe attracts everything else. In his time, this was a truly revolutionary concept.

Now, of course, the existence of gravity is universally acknowledged. In his theory of gravity, Newton observed that bodies with greater mass, such as planets and stars, have stronger gravity, or attraction, than do smaller bodies, such as asteroids.

The Sun has much greater mass than all other bodies in the solar system. Since it has the greatest gravity, it thus attracts the entire solar system and holds it in orbit.

Gravity keeps the *European Remote-sensing Satellite (ERS-1)*, and every other human-made satellite, in orbit around the Earth.

What's more, the gravity of a given mass extends endlessly into space. The Sun's gravity, for example, extends to Pluto, the outermost planet in the solar system, and far beyond. The gravity of stars inside gigantic clouds of gases, which may be a billion miles across, holds the clouds together and prevents their breaking apart.

Just as solar gravity holds the solar system in orbit, Earth's gravity holds its satellite, the Moon, in orbit. Earth's gravity also holds in orbit the space shuttles, the Russian space station named *Mir*, and the more than 2,000 human-made satellites that have been launched in the past half-century.

All of these bodies move rapidly through space. Human-made satellites and space shuttles travel about 18,000 miles (28,967 kilometers) per hour. As they travel, Earth's gravity attracts them, or pulls them toward the planet. Since they are pulled toward Earth, they do not travel in a straight line; rather,

Mass and Density

Which weighs more—a ton of feathers or a ton of steel? Of course, they weigh the same; a ton is a ton of whatever material. But which has greater density? Steel has, because the atomic particles that make up steel are packed more tightly together.

In the solar system, Earth, Mercury, Venus, Mars (and probably Pluto) are the densest planets. The material in them is packed close together. They are often called terrestrial planets—from the Latin word *terre*, meaning "Earth."

Jupiter, Saturn, Uranus, and Neptune are the giant gaseous planets. They all have low density, because their particles are not closely packed.

their path is curved, matching the curve of Earth's surface. If they are not going fast enough to resist the pull, they cannot remain in orbit. Earth's gravity then overcomes the orbital motion and pulls the satellites in toward its surface. These unmanned satellites burn up in Earth's atmosphere, or if large, parts of them crash somewhere on the planet.

Recent Theories About the Solar System

Today, we know that Copernicus was generally correct: The Earth moves around the Sun, and the Sun is the center of the solar system.

We also know that it is not just Earth that moves; the entire solar system moves. It travels as a unit in an orbit around the center of the Milky Way Galaxy. And, as the entire galaxy rotates, it travels through space.

What is more, the Milky Way is known to be a member of a group (termed the Local Group) of more than 20 galaxies that all hurtle through space together. This group of galaxies is part of a larger cluster of what may number thousands of galaxies. And this massive cluster may be part of a cluster of clusters. And numerous clusters of clusters may be part of larger structures called superclusters! Together, all these galaxies—perhaps 100 billion—make up the universe.

To further amaze all who study the secrets of space, it is possible that space may extend far beyond our own universe. In other words, there may be other universes that we have not yet discovered. We may never know for sure whether or not they exist. But many scientists think that they do.

Mass and Weight

Mass and weight are not the same thing. Mass is the amount of material, or matter, in a body—the Earth, the Sun, or you. Weight is a measure of the amount of gravity that is pulling on a mass.

Here on Earth, let's say that your mass is 100 pounds (45 kilograms). Your weight on Earth is also 100 pounds. This congruence, or equality, on Earth is why many people incorrectly believe that mass and weight are the same thing.

Suppose you traveled to the Moon. There, your weight would be much less, only about 16.5 pounds (7.5 kilograms)—one-sixth of your Earth-weight. This is because the gravitational force of the Moon is only one-sixth that of Earth. Your mass, however, would not change—it would still be 100 pounds.

On a space station orbiting in space, your mass would still be 100 pounds. Your weight, however, would be zero, or very close to it. That's because you would be in near-zero gravity. While the space station itself has mass and so exerts a gravitational force, this force is very small.

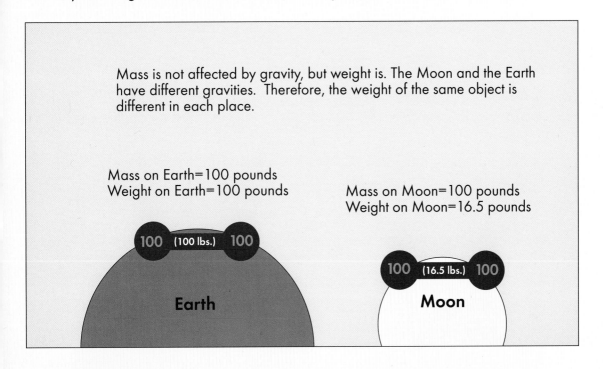

Mass is not affected by gravity, but weight is. The Moon and the Earth have different gravities. Therefore, the weight of the same object is different in each place.

Mass on Earth=100 pounds
Weight on Earth=100 pounds

100 (100 lbs.) 100

Earth

Mass on Moon=100 pounds
Weight on Moon=16.5 pounds

100 (16.5 lbs.) 100

Moon

A view of Earth rising over the Moon shows a blue, life-filled planet. We
do not yet know whether or not there is life on any other planet.

EARTH, THE MOON, AND OTHER SATELLITES

Earth is a most unusual planet in that it sustains life. On Earth, food grows and air is available to be used over and over again, as are water and soil. These—plus energy from the Sun—are all the necessities for life as we know it.

Earth is the third-closest planet to the Sun. Mercury and Venus are the two planets that are closer. Earth's distance from the Sun is just right for the emergence, development, and sustenance of life as we know it. A bit closer would be too hot; a bit farther out would be too cold.

As far as we know, there is no life anywhere else in the solar system. However, as we continue to learn what a small spot we occupy in the vast universe, many scientists and other people suggest that life may exist in places other than Earth. Organic molecules, the kind of particles that are associated with life, have been identified elsewhere in the Milky Way. And some people believe that they may have found organic molecules in meteorites that have fallen to Earth from outer space. But this has not been proven.

It is true that we have found no evidence of other life in the solar system, but we have not investigated all parts of it. Scientists do not have all the answers about the solar system, but there are many theories about it. For example, most astronomers believe that there are planets out among the stars still undiscovered. In fact, in 1995 and 1996, different groups of scientists in Switzerland and the United States found what they believe is evidence of previously unknown planets orbiting stars similar to our Sun. Could there, then, be other forms of life in our galaxy? Some argue that, if there are so many planets, it is likely that some of them have life-conducive conditions similar to those on Earth. At least one of the newly discovered celestial bodies appears to be the right temperature for water to exist—which means that life might be able to exist there! We may not be alone.

The Traveling Earth

Earth is always moving, as is everything else in the universe. Earth moves in many different ways, the main ones being rotation and revolution.

Earth has a diameter of 7,926 miles (12,756 kilometers), and the planet spins completely around in one day—to be precise, in 23 hours, 56 minutes, and 4.09 seconds.

How is one complete rotation measured? Suppose you are spinning in place. When you started spinning, a distant tree right in front of you would reappear in front of you after one complete rotation. That is the way Earth's rotation is measured. Instead of a tree, however, a point on Earth is lined up with a distant star—one that is so far away that the star has no apparent movement. When the point once again lines up with that star, one rotation is said to be complete. One day has passed. This is called a sidereal day; the word *sidereal* means "of the stars."

Now, suppose the point on Earth lines up with the Sun and begins its rotation. When the Sun once again is in line with the point, one day will have passed. This is called a solar day. It is four minutes longer than a sidereal day because, as Earth rotates, it is also going around the Sun. As viewed from Earth, the Sun appears to move among the background stars, an effect of our motion around the Sun. As Earth spins, the Sun "moves," and it takes four minutes for Earth to catch up to the Sun.

Earth spins around on its axis, much as a wheel spins around on an axle. The axis is not straight up and down; it is tilted 23.5° from the vertical. In June, July, and August, the Northern Hemisphere of Earth tilts toward the Sun, receiving a lot of solar energy. That is when it is summer in the Northern Hemisphere. During this season, Earth's arctic zone has continuous daylight, because it is constantly tilted toward the Sun. Six months later, during the Northern Hemisphere's

Seasons in the Northern Hemisphere

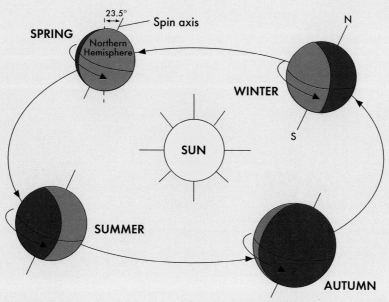

The 23.5° tilt of the Earth's axis toward the Sun means that in summer, not only is there more daylight, but the Sun's rays reach the Earth's surface more directly through the atmosphere and so lose less of their warmth. In winter, when the Earth is tilted away from the Sun, not only is there less daylight, but the Sun's rays have to pass through more of the Earth's atmosphere, losing more of their warmth.

winter, the northern half of Earth is tilted away from the Sun. Now the arctic region has continuous night and receives less energy from the Sun.

While Earth is rotating, it is also revolving around the Sun. It makes one complete revolution in about 365.25 days, what we call a year. Each Earth year, we complete a journey of 595 million miles (958 million kilometers). Amazingly, we do not feel our planet's motion, even though we are rotating at approximately 1,000 miles per hour (1,609 kilometers) and, at the same time, revolving around the Sun at a speed of nearly 66,600 miles (107,200 kilometers) per hour.

By watching other celestial bodies, though, we can perceive Earth's motion. As Earth revolves, it appears to us that the Sun is moving among the stars. No motion of the distant stars is apparent because they are so much farther away. Because of the Sun's apparent motion among the stars, we see changing star patterns in our night sky. These apparent star patterns, called constellations, change from summer to winter.

In the summer sky of the Northern Hemisphere, we see the constellations known as Cygnus (the swan), Scorpius (the scorpion), Aquila (the eagle), and Ophiuchus (the serpent-bearer). In winter in the Northern Hemisphere, Orion (the hunter) dominates the sky, and we can also see Gemini (the twins), Auriga (the charioteer), and Canis Major (the big dog). Today, stargazers recognize some 88 constellations.

Earth's Distance from the Sun

Earth's average distance from the Sun is about 93 million miles (150 million kilometers). In July, we are farther away—some 94,400,000 miles (152 million kilometers). In December and January, we are closer—approximately 91,300,000 miles (147 million kilometers). Distance from the Sun is a factor in our seasonal changes on Earth. But it is the tilt of Earth's axis that is the main cause of seasonal differences on Earth.

There is no big change of seasons on the Moon. Year in, year out, the seasons remain nearly the same. The Moon is very hot when in sunlight and very cold when in darkness.

The Moon is Earth's natural satellite. All of the planets except Mercury and Venus have satellites, or moons, that revolve around them—Pluto has one, Mars has two, there are at least

Most of the planets in our solar system have moons, but ours is one of the largest. It has a diameter of 2,160 miles (3,476 kilometers).

Landing on the Moon

On July 20, 1969, American astronaut Neil Armstrong stepped from the Lunar Lander, a part of *Apollo 11,* and put a foot on the Moon. He proclaimed it "one small step for a man, one giant leap for mankind." This was the first time that a human had been on the surface of any world other than Earth. Moments later, Edwin "Buzz" Aldrin followed Armstrong onto the surface of the Moon.

Five other successful missions to the Moon have since been made through a space-exploration program that is called *Apollo.* The *Apollo* program was created by the U.S. Space Agency, the National Aeronautics and Space Administration (NASA), headquartered in Houston, Texas.

The second lunar landing occurred just four months after the first. The third successful mission, in January 1971, brought back the largest amount of lunar material to date. During the fourth lunar landing, in July 1971, astronauts used a vehicle called the Lunar Rover for the first time. The fifth mission, in April 1972, set a new record for time spent on the Moon—a total of 20 hours and 14 minutes. And the last manned trip to the Moon, in December 1972, recovered about 243 pounds (110 kilograms) of lunar matter to be studied back on Earth.

Although we have now traveled to the Moon six times, it is never an easy trip to pull off. Being an astronaut is extremely dangerous. The original attempt at the third lunar mission, by *Apollo 13,* had to be aborted—cut short—in space when the spacecraft's oxygen tanks exploded. For a while, the survival of *Apollo 13* and the three astronauts traveling in it was touch-and-go. There was a good possibility that the spaceship would be destroyed or lose power, making it impossible to bring the ship back to Earth. If that had happened, the crew would have died, and the spaceship would have gone into an Earth-circling orbit. Finally, most of it would have burned up in Earth's atmosphere. Fortunately, the crew and NASA were able to bring the ship safely back to Earth.

16 around Jupiter, 17 around Saturn, Uranus has at least 15, and Neptune has at least 8. The planets with gaseous rings have the most satellites; the two planets closest to the Sun have none. More satellites may be discovered as space research progresses.

Our Moon has a diameter of 2,160 miles (3,476 kilometers) and is one of the larger moons in the solar system. The Moon rotates in the same amount of time that it revolves around the Earth—exactly 27 days, 7 hours, 43 minutes, and 11.47 seconds. As a result, the same half, or hemisphere, of the Moon always faces toward us. We did not see the other side of the Moon until 1959, when lunar probes with cameras aboard went around the "far side" of the Moon, took pictures, and sent them back to Earth.

Like Earth, the Moon is made of space debris. So are all of the other satellites, the comets, the meteoroids, and the asteroids. The Moon was probably formed out of the same cloud that was the origin of the Sun, Earth, and the other planets.

The materials found on the Moon are the same as those found on Earth. However, the percentages of the various elements, such as iron, silicon, and oxygen, are not the same. That is likely because the different substances in the original gas cloud were not distributed evenly throughout the cloud. This would also account for the great variations in the percentages of different materials in the planets.

As the lunar materials consolidated, their temperature went up rapidly. Volcanoes developed, breaking through the Moon's outer surface, which had solidified earlier. Even though those volcanoes became extinct billions of years ago, many of their craters still exist. Today, the Moon is covered with craters and

Eclipses

The Moon always casts a shadow. When the Moon gets in line between the Sun and Earth, the tip of its shadow, called a shadow cone, may fall on a region of Earth. When that happens, the Moon blocks the Sun from that region. This is called a total eclipse of the Sun. In the region where the Moon's partial shadow falls, however, only part of the eclipse is seen.

If the shadow cone does not quite reach Earth, there is an annular eclipse. In an annular eclipse, a thin ring of the Sun rims the Moon (an annulus is a ring).

Earth also casts a shadow. When Earth is between the Sun and the Moon, Earth's shadow cone reaches the Moon. As the Moon moves into this cone, there is a lunar eclipse, meaning that the Moon can be viewed only very faintly from some parts of Earth. Eclipses of the Moon occur each year, as do solar eclipses. Because only a small part of the Earth is in the lunar (Moon) shadow at a given time, however, there is a long lapse between total solar eclipses at any single location. For example, people in New York City witnessed a total solar eclipse in 1925; the next time a total solar eclipse will be visible there is in the year 2024.

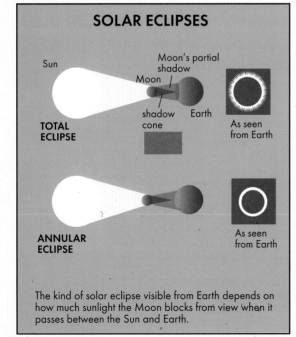

SOLAR ECLIPSES

Sun

Moon's partial shadow

Moon

shadow cone

Earth

TOTAL ECLIPSE

As seen from Earth

ANNULAR ECLIPSE

As seen from Earth

The kind of solar eclipse visible from Earth depends on how much sunlight the Moon blocks from view when it passes between the Sun and Earth.

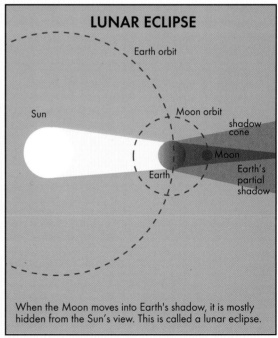

LUNAR ECLIPSE

Earth orbit

Sun

Moon orbit

shadow cone

Moon

Earth

Earth's partial shadow

When the Moon moves into Earth's shadow, it is mostly hidden from the Sun's view. This is called a lunar eclipse.

lava fields. They remain much as they were when they first formed because there is no wind or water on the Moon to erode them.

Meteorites, Meteoroids, Asteroids, and Comets

Space is far from empty. A large part of the meteoric dust in space is left behind by the passage of comets. When Earth moves through a comet's orbit, the planet sweeps up the debris. Every day, about 1,000 tons (910 metric tons) of meteoric material fall on Earth.

A meteoroid is a space particle, while a meteorite is a type of meteoroid that lands on Earth. As many as 3,000 meteorites fall to Earth each year. A meteor is the trail of light that is made as a meteoroid streaks through Earth's atmosphere.

Most meteoroids are very small—the size of a grain of sand. But some can be quite large, perhaps the size of a football or baseball. Meteorites have struck animals and people on rare occasions. One such incident occurred in Sylacauga, Alabama, when a meteorite weighing about ten pounds (4.5 kilograms) crashed through the roof and then the ceiling and struck a surprised Mrs. Hewlett Hodges on her leg. In 1971, a meteorite weighing about a pound went through another person's roof and embedded in the ceiling. Despite these unusual stories, there is no reason to worry about being hit by a meteorite because the chances of this happening are extremely remote. When you're outside, however, meteorite dust probably falls on you constantly.

Asteroids are larger meteoroids that travel mostly between the orbits of Mars and Jupiter. The largest asteroid, named

Halley's Comet was discovered by Edmund Halley in 1910 and was seen again in 1986, when this picture was taken.

Ceres, measures about 600 miles (966 kilometers) across. Very rarely, asteroids may come near Earth.

Comets consist mostly of gases, but they have a small, solid core. Comets move in long and narrow elliptical orbits. As a comet orbits closer and closer to the Sun, it develops a "tail" as the ice that makes up most of it vaporizes into space. There are probably millions of comets that we never see from Earth. Occasionally, however, one comes near enough so we can see what has been described as a "hairy star" in our night skies.

Signs of a comet collision with Earth have been found in Siberia. Scientists believe that, in 1908, a great comet flattened entire forests there and caused widespread destruction. Some scientists believe that a comet crashing into Earth may have killed the dinosaurs. The only other known comet collision was that of Shoemaker-Levy 9 with Jupiter in 1994, an event that is called the most violent recorded event in the history of the solar system.

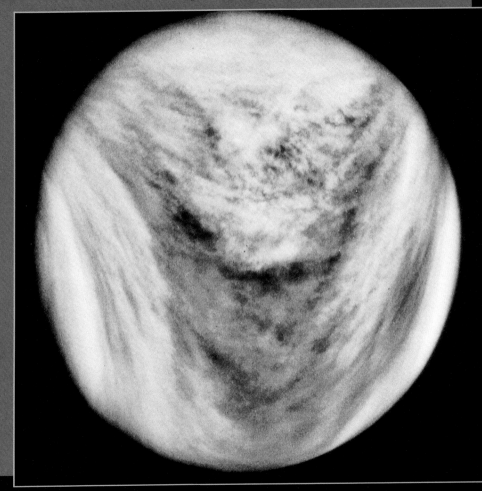

The first Venus orbiter took this ultraviolet photo of clouds over Venus.

CHAPTER 4

THE INNER PLANETS

Mercury, Venus, and Mars, along with Earth, are referred to as terrestrial planets because they have high densities and rocky surfaces. They are also called the inner planets, as they are closer to the Sun than the other five planets in our solar system. The inner planets also lie inside the asteroid belt.

The Planet Closest to the Sun

Mercury has been known since ancient times because it can sometimes be seen with the naked eye, unaided by a telescope. The second-smallest planet, Mercury has a diameter of only 3,031 miles (4,878 kilometers), less than half the diameter of Earth. As it is only about 36 million miles (58 million kilometers) from the Sun, Mercury is very hot. Named for the Roman "winged messenger" of the gods, Mercury moves quickly around the Sun. It averages about 107,000 miles (172,195 kilometers) per hour and completes one revolution in 88 days, exposing all of its surface to the Sun. The sunlit side of Mercury can reach 806°F (430°C).

Mercury's path around the Sun has a more elliptical shape than any other planet. And, unlike most of the other planets in our solar system that travel at a tilt, Mercury orbits upright. There are no known moons or rings of Mercury.

There is some dispute over whether or not Mercury has a thin carbon dioxide atmosphere. Nighttime temperatures of both 70°F and -292°F (21°C and -180°C) have been reported by researchers—extreme differences in data that cause scientists to be unsure of the makeup of Mercury's atmosphere.

In 1974 and 1975, *Mariner 10* passed by Mercury three times and was able to photograph about 57 percent of the planet's

Mercury—the small dark spot—is shown crossing in front of the Sun.

surface. These photographs showed many craterlike formations, similar to those on the Moon. These, and thousands of others, were probably made during the showers of debris soon after the formation of the solar system. Ancient lava flows have smoothed over many of the craters. This indicates volcanic activity on Mercury.

One unique feature that has been mapped is the Caloris Basin, a large crater that is 808 miles (1,300 kilometers) in diameter. Scientists believe this was probably created when a chunk of rock from space crashed into the planet. The impact was so strong that hills were pushed up on the other side of the crater! Data from the *Mariner 10* expedition also showed that Mercury has a weak, but permanent, magnetic field. No space probe has visited Mercury since the *Mariner 10*. Many of the mysteries of this planet closest to the Sun remain unsolved.

Venus and Earth Compared

If you could live on Venus, you would have no concern about seasons because they are not very noticeable there. Conditions on the planet are nearly the same year in and year out. Venus is not the closest planet to the Sun, but even so, its sunlit side reaches extremely hot temperatures—up to 869°F (465°C). A hot cooking oven can rise to 500°F (260°C)—you would cook in a hurry if you ever landed on Venus!

You would probably be killed first by the atmosphere, however. Venus's atmosphere is about 96.5 percent carbon dioxide and 3.5 percent nitrogen, as well as minor amounts of oxygen, water, and sulfur compounds. You could not survive in it for very long.

Clearly, the temperature and atmosphere of Venus are formidable foes to life as we know it. This reality is very different from the way people have thought about the planet through the centuries. Venus has been considered the queen of the planets because of its bright glow in our skies. It has also been called Earth's twin because its diameter is nearly the same as Earth's. The diameter of Venus is 7,520 miles (12,102 kilometers), while that of Earth is 7,926 miles (12,756 kilometers).

Aside from their diameters, the two planets are certainly not twinlike. Venus moves much faster in its orbit around the Sun than Earth does. Venus travels 78,192 miles (127,457 kilometers) an hour, while Earth goes 66,600 miles (107,200 kilometers) an hour. A revolution of Venus around the Sun takes only 225 days. This is because Venus is closer to the Sun than is Earth, which, as we have mentioned, completes a revolution around the Sun in about 365.25 days. In addition, Venus rotates relatively slowly, taking approximately 243 days to spin completely around once, while Earth takes only 23 hours and 56 minutes.

The View of Venus from Earth

Venus sometimes appears to glow brightly in our evening skies. At other times, it appears as a bright point of light in our morning skies. For centuries before people learned more about astronomy, it was believed that Venus was actually two different stars, an evening star and a morning star. The evening "star" was called Hesperus, and the morning "star" was named Phosphorous—Greek words meaning "western" and "bringer of light."

The orbit of Venus is "inside" Earth's orbit; that is, Venus is closer to the Sun than Earth is. As a result, sometimes Venus appears to the east of the Sun—and is a morning object. At other times, it is west of the Sun—and is an evening point of light.

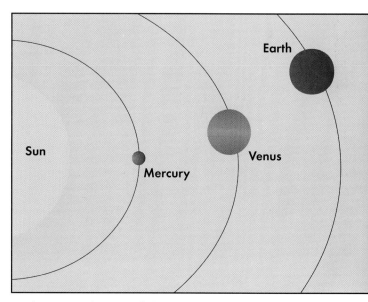

In this partial view of the solar system, Venus is shown to be "inside" Earth's orbit.

Venus was an early target for planet probes. Previously, its solid surface was difficult to see, as it is completely covered with clouds. Whenever people looked at Venus, all they saw was sunlight reflecting off the clouds, much like a mirror. This ability to reflect causes Venus to appear to us as the third-brightest object in the sky, after the Sun and the Moon.

In 1962, the United States sent the *Mariner 2* probe to learn more about Venus. In 1967 and 1969, more data were gathered by the Soviet Union, using probes *Venera 4* and *Venera 5*. Several other successful missions were completed in the year after that. But the most eye-opening journey to Venus took place in 1989.

On May 4, 1989, the unmanned planet probe *Magellan* was launched from the shuttle *Atlantis* into orbit around Venus. The probe was equipped with radar. The radar waves were able to penetrate the planet's atmosphere, and they bounced from the surface back to *Magellan* in a mere microsecond.

The radar waves were used to assemble a map of 98 percent of the planet. This map shows that, on Venus, there are lowland basins and highland areas. The surface of Venus is uneven.

Here, Venus appears as an evening star along with the Moon.

There are craters that were produced in the early days of the planet, when huge meteorites crashed into the surface.

At many locations on Venus, there are lava fields produced by ancient volcanoes. Many of the volcanic cones still exist, probably because there is no rain on Venus to erode them. Here on Earth, falling water and flowing streams wear down mountains and carry the pulverized rock, or sand, into ocean basins. The effect is a slow leveling of the Earth's surface over millions of years.

The Red Planet

We know more about Mars than any other planet except Earth. The conditions on Mars are opposite those on Venus. Mars is extremely cold and has a thin atmosphere, made up mostly of carbon dioxide. There are also traces of oxygen, ozone, and argon. Mars has two satellites, or moons, called Deimos and Phobos. It is believed that the orbit of Phobos is slowly circling downward and that the moon will crash into the surface of Mars in about 30 million years.

With a diameter of 4,223 miles (6,796 kilometers), Mars is slightly more than half the size of Earth. Like Earth and all of the other planets, Mars rotates. Mars takes 24 hours, 37 minutes, about the same time that Earth takes, to spin once. It revolves around the Sun once every 687 days. The surface of Mars is full of craters and volcanoes. One volcano, called Olympus Mons, is higher than Mt. Everest. In fact, at 79,200 to 84,480 feet (24,140 to 25,750 meters), it is the highest mountain known in the solar system! There is also a canyon, the Valles Marineris, that is 2,796 to 3,107 miles (4,500 to 5,000 kilometers) long and up to 373 miles (600 kilometers) wide, many times the size of the Grand Canyon. The presence of dry stream beds suggests that, at one time, Mars had quite a lot of water that eroded its topography.

The planet is about 142 million miles (228 million kilometers) from the Sun (although its non-circular orbit causes that number to vary significantly), as compared to Earth's distance of 93 million miles (150 million kilometers). Mars, therefore, receives much less solar energy than Earth does. And it does not retain the heat that it does receive because the planet's atmosphere is very thin. In daytime, the "hot" regions of Mars may reach 72°F (22°C). At night, the same regions can drop to -207°F (-133°C).

Mariner 9, which orbited Mars in 1971, was responsible for much of the information that we have about Mars today, transmitting some 7,000 pictures of Mars back to Earth. The success of the *Mariner 9* mission led to the *Viking 1* and *Viking 2* landings on the surface of Mars in 1976. One of the landers was equipped with devices that found considerable iron on the planet—as

Viking 1 and *Viking 2* found great amounts of iron in the rocky landscape on Mars. This photo was taken from *Viking 1*.

well as other rocks and materials, such as sand, which contains a lot of silicon. (Earth's beach sand is mostly silicon dioxide.) The other *Viking* probe looked for signs of life existing on Mars or relics of past life. All results were negative.

Mars continues to be of great interest to scientists, and so the NASA space program includes plans to send more Mars landers to explore the surface. A new project called the Mars Environmental Survey (MESUR) will send the rover *Pathfinder* to continue to explore Mars and expand our knowledge of the planet.

The Canals

At the end of the nineteenth century, there was little doubt among many people that there was intelligent life on Mars. An Italian astronomer named Giovanni Schiaparelli reported in

1877 that he had seen "canali" on Mars, through a telescope. People immediately believed there were canals on the planet, even though Schiaparelli never said that. He used the word *canali*, which in Italian means "channels." Channels could be made naturally, while canals would have to be built by intelligent creatures. People seemed to focus on the idea of canals, however, and misunderstood Schiaparelli's observations.

In the late 1800s, Percival Lowell, an American astronomer and a wealthy businessman, became fascinated by the idea of people on Mars. He built an observatory in Arizona in order to get a better look at the planet.

What Lowell saw convinced him that there were indeed canals—human-made structures—on Mars. He reported that there were 500 canals carrying water from the ice caps of the planet toward its equator. He was sure of this because he could see green areas appear seasonally in the warmer regions of Mars as the ice cap melted. He argued that water carried by the canals made things grow.

As stronger telescopes were developed and used, the "canals" of Mars turned out to be surface features that were parallel to each other and so looked like channels. And today, the "green" regions are believed to be patterns made when sand of different colors is blown about and mixed together.

In spite of its life-hostile conditions, some people believe that we will eventually build a colony on Mars. Some suggest that we will be able to grow plants on the planet, which will gradually remove poisons from the atmosphere of Mars. After many centuries, some say, Mars will be able to support people much as Earth does.

The Voyager spacecraft heads toward Jupiter and Saturn, the two largest planets in our solar system.

CHAPTER 5

THE OUTER PLANETS

Beyond Mars lie the five outer planets. Four of these are the so-called gas giants—Jupiter, Saturn, Uranus, and Neptune. They are much larger than the terrestrial planets and are huge spheres of hydrogen and other gases. The fifth, in contrast, is Pluto, the smallest known planet. The outer planets are so named because they are farther from the Sun than the inner cluster and lie outside the asteroid belt.

The Greatest Gas Giant

Jupiter was the greatest of the Roman gods, and it is the greatest of all the planets. It is so large that 300 Earths could fit inside it. The diameter of the planet is 88,846 miles (142,984 kilometers)—11.2 times the diameter of Earth. Jupiter's speed of rotation is very fast. A day on Jupiter is just under 10 hours long, but it takes almost 12 Earth years for Jupiter to make one revolution around the Sun. The planet is a lot farther from the Sun than is Earth—approximately 484 million miles (779 million kilometers) away—so it is very cold. Its average surface temperature is -238°F (-150°C). Jupiter has one thin ring, 0.6 mile (0.97 kilometer) in thickness.

The gases of Jupiter's atmosphere surround a relatively small solid core. Thousands of miles deep, these gases are made up of hydrogen, helium, methane, ammonia, ethane, and small amounts of other gases. Jupiter's atmosphere is a very colorful one and has the appearance of having many stripes running parallel to its equator. Gray or brown stripes called belts alternate with lighter stripes called zones. A whiff or two of the atmosphere on Jupiter would be your last. Therefore, nobody anticipates landing on Jupiter. However, unmanned probes will continue to be sent to learn more about its atmosphere.

As viewed from Earth, Jupiter's cloud surface is always changing, indicating that the gases are mixing and whirling about. Yet one enormous region, called the Great Red Spot, has been

The *Galileo* Probe

The *Galileo* probe began its exploration of Jupiter, the solar system's biggest planet, in December 1995. The probe is named after Galileo Galilei, who discovered four of Jupiter's moons in 1610. *Galileo* will enable scientists to study the composition of Jupiter and its 16 moons for almost two years. This unmanned probe was carried into space by the shuttle *Atlantis* and was launched toward Jupiter on October 18, 1989. It took six years for *Galileo* to reach Jupiter on December 7, 1995. On its journey there, *Galileo* passed an asteroid at a distance of 1,000 miles (1,609 kilometers) and took the first close-up photograph of an asteroid in space.

Jupiter's Great Red Spot is an atmospheric storm that rotates counter-clockwise. It has been observed for at least three centuries.

seen for at least three centuries. The Great Red Spot would cover three Earths. It is an atmospheric storm that rotates counter-clockwise at the outer edge but has almost no movement at all at the center. *Voyager I* and *Voyager II* showed that the Great Red Spot may hover higher than the clouds. Its color and size have changed over the years.

In 1994, Jupiter made the headlines because a comet was heading for the planet. The event aroused much interest since some people had been speculating that it was entirely possible that a comet or a meteoroid would at some time strike Earth. The comet that was hurtling toward Jupiter was named Shoemaker-Levy 9, after Eugene and Carolyn Shoemaker and David Levy, who discovered it. When the comet reached Jupiter, it broke into 20 fragments. One after the other, these fragments crashed into the atmosphere of the planet, from July 16 to

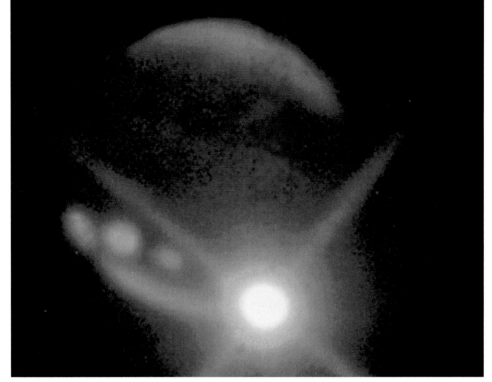

A fireball is created as a fragment of Comet Shoemaker-Levy 9 hits Jupiter. Earlier sites of impact can be seen as glowing spots on the right.

July 22, 1994. These impacts caused great explosions that must have been tremendous, for they could easily be seen through telescopes from Earth—almost half a billion miles away.

The explosions left large, dark impact points that seem to be high up in Jupiter's atmosphere, because the stripes of the planet can be seen through them. Questions have surfaced regarding the S-L-9 comet and the possibility that it was really an asteroid, but answers may not be determined for years.

The Ringed Planet

Saturn is the second-largest planet in the solar system. It is also the least dense. If there were an ocean large enough to hold it, Saturn would float. This planet has a diameter of 74,898 miles

(120,536 kilometers). Its rotation is about 10 and a half hours, and it takes 29.5 Earth years to complete a revolution around the Sun. Saturn's atmospheric appearance is similar to Jupiter's, with swirls and dark and light markings. *Voyager 1* and *Voyager 2* have measured winds of 1,120 miles (1,802 kilometers) per hour near Saturn's equator. In comparison, some of the strongest and most destructive winds to blow on Earth were those of Hurricane Andrew in 1992, which had speeds of up to 165 miles (265 kilometers) per hour.

Saturn is beautiful to view, especially when its rings are visible. Sometimes, they are edge-on and so cannot be seen. For a long time, the rings that encircle Saturn were the only ones known in the solar system. Now, we know that Jupiter, Uranus, and Neptune also have rings; however, Saturn is still the only known planet to have an intricate ring system.

Until 1979, Saturn was known to have ten satellites, or moons. But in September of that year, *Pioneer 11* passed the planet and

A view of Saturn as *Pioneer 11* finishes its encounter with the planet.

saw a few more. Its cameras did not get very good pictures, though. Later, *Voyager 1*, in 1980, and *Voyager 2*, in 1981, retrieved data indicating that Saturn has from 18 to 23 moons. In May 1995, the Hubble Space Telescope was able to observe two previously unknown moons.

A Planet on Its Side

It once was believed that Saturn was the outermost planet in the solar system. Then, in 1781, William Herschel, a German-English astronomer, discovered Uranus. It is the seventh planet from the Sun. This was a remarkable discovery, for although Herschel had a telescope that was powerful for the technology of the time, it was in no way comparable to telescopes today. It has been said that to Herschel, Uranus probably looked no larger than a pea would look at a distance of two football fields. Yet Herschel knew it was a planet because of the way that it moved against the background stars.

In 1986, *Voyager 2* moved in close to Uranus and got the best view yet of the planet.

The rings of Uranus can be seen in this view of the planet taken from above its moon, Miranda.

It was able to verify the existence of nine rings of Uranus and identify two new ones. Uranus has at least 15 moons. One is named Miranda and has been called "the most bizarre body in the solar system." Miranda has an extremely complex geologic surface, with rolling, heavily cratered plains, canyons, and what appear to be three enormous oval-shaped areas.

Perhaps the strangest thing about Uranus is the tilt of its axis. Earth's axis is tilted 23.5° from the vertical, but the axis of Uranus is tilted 98°—the planet leans way over on its side. Because of the way it is tilted, the north pole of the planet is pointed toward the Sun for some 42 years; and 42 years later, sunlight falls in the planet's south pole. The planet takes about 84 years to go around the Sun. Uranus would be a very difficult place to explore, as it is subfreezing cold. The overall temperature is about -346°F (-210°C).

The Smallest Giant

People who charted the motions of Uranus in the years after its discovery concluded that the planet was not moving in a predictable way. It seemed like the gravity of some nearby object was affecting the planet's movements. Could there be another planet out beyond Uranus?

In 1846, some 65 years after the discovery of Uranus, another planet was discovered. John Couch Adams, an Englishman, figured out where the planet should be, but he did not have a telescope. At the same time, a Frenchman, Urbain Le Verrier, also calculated where the new planet should be. But he had no telescope either. Le Verrier told Johann Galle what his figures indicated. Galle, an astronomer at the Berlin Observatory,

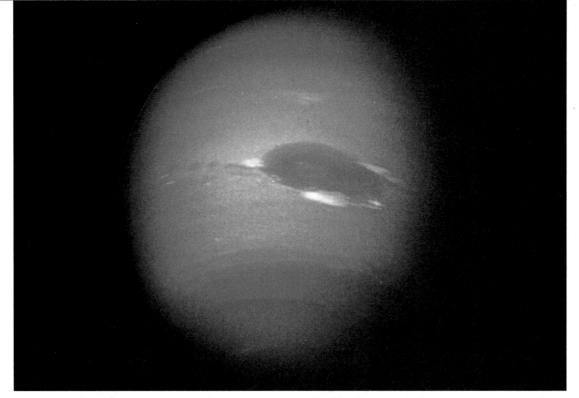

Neptune's atmosphere is composed of hydrogen, helium, ammonia, and methane. The methane gives it a blue appearance.

turned his telescope to that part of the sky and became the first person to see Neptune. All three men, however, are credited with the discovery.

Since its discovery in 1846, little was known about Neptune until *Voyager 2* flew past it in August 1989. This was the first time a spacecraft had passed Neptune—and it traveled as close as 3,000 miles (4,827 kilometers) above Neptune's north pole. It also passed by Neptune's largest moon, Triton, at a distance of about 25,000 miles (40,225 kilometers), and it discovered six other moons. From the information *Voyager 2* gathered, we are now aware of eight satellites of Neptune and four rings.

Neptune orbits the Sun once approximately every 165 years and is about 2.8 billion miles (4.5 billion kilometers) away from the Sun. It has a diameter of 30,775 miles (49,517 kilometers), which makes it the smallest of the four gas giants. However, Neptune, Jupiter, Saturn, and Uranus are all 4 to 11 times greater than Earth in diameter.

Neptune has some interesting characteristics, one of which is a storm center similar to Jupiter's Great Red Spot. Near this storm, called the Great Dark Spot, *Voyager 2* measured winds up to 1,250 miles (2,012 kilometers) per hour—the strongest winds measured on any planet to date.

Farthest from the Sun?

Pluto was discovered in 1930 by Clyde Tombaugh, who was hired by the Lowell Observatory in Tucson, Arizona, to hunt for the planet even before he was an astronomer. He got the job because he had studied the subject for a long time and was excited by the quest.

Pluto is extremely cold all the time. Its mean surface temperature is -364°F (-220°C) because it is so far from the Sun, averaging approximately 3.7 billion miles (5.9 billion kilometers) away. It was previously thought that the order of the planets in the solar system was static; that is, that the planets did not change in relationship to the Sun. Pluto has long been known as the planet farthest from the Sun. However, Pluto's orbit varies so much that it can sometimes be only 2.7 billion miles (4.4 billion kilometers) away from the Sun. When that is the case, as it has been since 1989 and will be until 1999, Neptune is actually the planet farthest from the Sun.

The discovery of Pluto in 1930 occurred about 35 years after its existence was theorized by the astronomer Percival Lowell, for whom the Lowell Observatory is named. His prediction was based on the theory that there was a planet beyond Neptune and Uranus that was affecting their orbits. The planet's name, Pluto, was based on Percival Lowell's initials.

In 1978, a photograph of Pluto was taken by James Christy at the U.S. Naval Observatory in Flagstaff. The photograph clearly showed that Pluto's shape was elongated. The variations of Pluto's shape continued to be studied, and scientists became convinced that Pluto must have a satellite. This satellite, named Charon, was subsequently discovered and shown to be 12,204 miles (19,640 kilometers) from Pluto. Pluto and Charon seem to revolve together as one system. A plan to send spacecraft to observe the Pluto-Charon system, to be called the *Pluto Express*, is being considered by NASA.

Pluto's diameter is 1,423 miles (2,290 kilometers). Pluto's surface appears to be frozen methane. This methane may be slowly escaping into space and possibly traveling to Charon. Pluto may also have polar caps—observations have shown that the planet has large regions that are dark and others that are light.

In recent years, some astronomers have argued that Pluto is too small and has too variable an orbit to be a planet. Most scientists, however, are convinced that it is, as it has the basic characteristics of a planet—it is round, it has an atmosphere, and it has a moon.

....

For all of the information that we have gathered about our solar system, it seems clear that we have only scratched the surface. Many secrets of space still elude us. But as our technologies continue to develop, so will our knowledge of the vast universe in which we live.

Fast Facts About the Planets

Planet	Mercury	Venus	Earth	Mars	Jupiter	Saturn	Uranus	Neptune	Pluto
Approximate distance from Sun:									
in miles	36 million	67 million	93 million	142 million	484 million	886 million	1.7 billion	2.8 billion	3.6 billion
in kilometers	58 million	108 million	150 million	228 million	779 million	1.4 billion	2.8 billion	4.5 billion	5.8 billion
Revolution period, in Earth years	0.24	0.6	1.0	1.8	11.9	29.4	84.01	164.8	247.7
Rotation, in Earth hours	1,408	5,832	23.9	24.6	9.9	10.6	17.2	16.1	153.3
Diameter:									
in miles	3,031	7,520	7,926	4,217	88,849	74,978	31,022	30,775	1,423
in kilometers	4,878	12,100	12,753	6,785	142,958	120,640	49,946	49,517	2,290
Main composition of the surface	Rock	Rock	Rock, water, water ice	Rock, carbon dioxide ice, water ice	Gaseous	Gaseous	Gaseous	Gaseous	Nitrogen ice, water ice, carbon dioxide ice
Main composition of the atmosphere	Unclear; perhaps carbon dioxide	Carbon dioxide, nitrogen	Nitrogen, oxygen, water	Carbon dioxide	Hydrogen, helium, methane, ammonia	Hydrogen, helium, methane, ammonia	Hydrogen, helium, methane	Hydrogen, helium, methane	Nitrogen
Moons	0	0	1	2	at least 16	17–23	at least 15	at least 8	1
Rings	0	0	0	0	1	Thousands	11	5	Unknown

GLOSSARY

annular eclipse A solar eclipse during which the Sun appears blotted out by the Moon, except for a bright ring around it.

asteroid A large meteoroid; most travel between the orbits of Mars and Jupiter.

atom The smallest particle of a chemical element that has the chemical properties of that element.

axis An imaginary line around which a body, such as a planet, rotates.

Big Bang A theory that explains the origin and evolution of the universe, starting with a cataclysmic explosion.

cluster A group of things of the same kind situated together.

comet A bright, heavenly body made up of frozen gases, ice, and dust particles.

constellation A group of stars forming a pattern.

corona The outer atmosphere of the Sun, seen as a ring of light during an eclipse.

cosmic cloud A huge cloud of gases (largely hydrogen) in outer space.

cosmic fireball What resulted when the original supercore of the universe exploded.

diameter The length across an object, measured through the center.

eclipse A partial or total darkening of a planet, Moon, or Sun.

galaxy A vast grouping of stars, planets, satellites, meteors, dust, and gases.

geocentric Earth-centered; the idea that the Earth is the center of the solar system.

heliocentric Sun-centered; the idea that the Sun is the center of the solar system.

light-year The distance that light travels through space in one year, or 5,878 trillion miles (9,459 trillion kilometers).

mass A property of matter.

meteor A streak of light that is made by a meteoroid.

meteoroid A solid particle flying through space—it is usually very small, even microscopic.

meteorite A meteoroid that has landed on Earth.

probe An unmanned spacecraft used to explore space.

rotation Spinning around on an axis.

revolution The movement of one body around another, such as the Earth revolving around the Sun.

sidereal Measured by means of stars.

satellite A celestial or human-made object that orbits another larger body, such as a planet; the Moon is Earth's natural satellite.

star A heavenly body that shines by its own light, as distinguished from planets and their satellites, comets, and meteors.

weight The quality of any mass or body that is a result of the pull of gravity upon it.

Brandt, Keith. *Planets and the Solar System*. Mahwah, NJ: Troll, 1985.

Branley, Franklyn M. *Jupiter*. New York: Elsevier Science, Inc., 1981.

————. *Keeping Time*. New York: Houghton-Mifflin, 1993.

————. *Neptune*. New York: HarperCollins, 1992.

————. *Saturn*. New York: HarperCollins, 1983.

————. *Uranus*. New York: HarperCollins, 1988.

————. *Venus*. New York: HarperCollins, 1994.

Cooper, Heather, and Nigel Henbest. *How the Universe Works*. Pleasantville, NY: Readers Digest, 1994.

Fradin, Dennis B. *Astronomy*. Chicago: Children's Press, 1987.

Kerrod, Robin. *The Solar System*. New York: Marshall Cavendish, 1993.

Moché, Dinah L. *Astronomy Today*. New York: Random House, 1982.

Verba, Joan M. *Voyager: Exploring the Outer Planets*. Minneapolis, MN: Lerner, 1991.

Vogt, Gregory L. *The Solar System: Facts and Exploration*. New York: Twenty-First Century Books, 1995.

ON-LINE

The home page for *The Universe at Our Doorstep* lets you access all kinds of information about the solar system, space travel, space research, and more. Browse through its library at http://neptune.cgy.oanet.com/

On-line telescopes link you to automated telescopes on the Internet. Some allow you to actually use the telescopes; others let you find out about them. Contact them at http://www.eia.brad.ac.uk/rti/automated.html

SOURCES

Beatty, J. Kelly, and Andrew Chaikin, Editors. *The New Solar System.* Cambridge, MA: Sky Publishing, 1990.

Curtis, Anthony E., Editor. *Space Almanac.* Houston: Gulf Publishing Company, 1992.

Hawking, Stephen. *A Brief History of Time.* New York: Bantam Books, 1988.

Kelley, Kevin W., Editor. *The Home Planet.* Reading, MA: Addison-Wesley, 1988.

Lederman, Leon, and David Schramm. *From Quarks to the Cosmos.* Scientific American Library, 1989.

Zeilik, Michael. *Astronomy: The Evolving Universe.* New York: HarperCollins, 1982.

INDEX